Potpourri

A FRIEDMAN GROUP BOOK

Copyright © 1991 by Michael Friedman Publishing Group, Inc.

First published in Canada in 1991 by Doubleday Canada Limited.

Canadian Cataloguing in Publication Data

Randolph, Barbara
Potpourri

Includes index.
ISBN 0-385-25334-6

1. Potpourris (Scented floral mixtures). I. Title.

TT889.4.R63 1991   745.92   C91-093787-7

POTPOURRI
was prepared and produced by
Michael Friedman Publishing Group, Inc.
15 West 26th Street
New York, New York 10010

Editor: Sharon Kalman
Designer: Devorah Levinrad
Photography Editor: Christopher C. Bain

Typeset by Bookworks Plus
Color separation by Excel Graphic Arts Ltd.
Printed and bound in Hong Kong by Leefung-Asco Printers Ltd.

Published in Canada by
Doubleday Canada Limited
105 Bond Street
Toronto, Ontario
M5B 1Y3

Potpourri

♦ ♦ ♦ ♦ ♦

Barbara Randolph

Photography by Jennifer Lévy

Doubleday Canada Limited, Toronto

Contents

Introduction

◊ ◊ ◊ ◊ ◊

The scents of a summer garden are among life's most elusive treasures. While you can't quite bottle the smell of the evening breeze, it is surprisingly easy to keep some of the season's gentle fragrances in a potpourri jar.

Creating fragrant and beautiful blends of flowers, herbs, and spices is both an art and a science, but it can also be a hobby whose greatest successes are serendipitous. There are no rules about which herbs and flowers go together. If your nose and your eyes tell you it is right, then it is.

Creating fragrances with flowers and herbs is a pleasure that anyone can enjoy. Although a backyard garden provides a ready source of materials, those without a garden can have just as much fun creating their own blends. Natural food stores, fragrance shops, herb farms, florists, and mail-order suppliers sell everything necessary to create beautiful, fragrant potpourri. Some of the ingredients can be gathered in the wild from roadsides, the seashore, or even vacant lots.

So read on; you will be creating your own original potpourri before you know it.

P·O·T·P·O·U·R·R·I B·A·S·I·C·S

The Ingredients

While scent is the most important consideration in making any potpourri, it is not the only one. Color is important if the blend is to be displayed in an open container or glass jar. For this reason, whole perfect blossoms add interesting highlights.

Fragrances need room if they are to blend and mellow properly, so some ingredients in each potpourri should provide bulk. Large flowers such as marigolds, zinnias, celosia, strawflowers, and globe amaranth serve this purpose well, adding bright colors at the same time.

Before preparing the potpourri all ingredients should be thoroughly dry. Leaves should snap or crumble when bent or rubbed. If the ingredients are still moist, the blend is likely to mildew when it is sealed in a jar.

There are a number of synthetic and dyed materials available for making potpourri. These are often less expensive than natural materials, but they are also not as good. Dyed woodchips that have been permeated with oils look and smell artificial. The colors are usually too bright. The same is true of dried flowers that have been dyed. There may be occasions when these are all you can get in certain colors, but use them sparingly if you use them at all.

Note: The ◊ indicates potpourri basics, used most often for either their scent or appearance, or both.

Acacia: Small gray-green leaves and the tips of twigs. Acacia has a slightly woody scent that blends well with nearly anything.

◊ *Allspice:* Brown berries, larger than peppercorns, with a distinct spicy fragrance. In potpourri they are used whole, rather than in the powdered form used for cooking.

Artemisia, Silver King or Silver Queen: Only faintly fragrant, their gray leaves are used for color. They blend especially well with shades of pink and rose.

Baby's breath: White or pale pink with tiny flowers and no fragrance. The varieties with larger flowers show up best in potpourri. Available fresh or dried from florists.

◊ *Balsam fir:* The needles and tips from this particular variety of fir tree are very strongly scented. They retain a good shade of green if the branches are removed from the tree and dried in a cool, shady place. If you are lucky enough to have access to balsam Christmas trees, save the needles and tips. Needles of other conifers are not a substitute. Although the cones of the balsam tree have very little scent, they are small and attractive.

◊ *Bay leaves:* Olive green when dried, with a delicate fragrance. You may use the same bay leaves you use in cooking, but the wild bay that grows along the shore has an equally pleasant fragrance.

Birchbark: White curls of outer bark from the white birch. Although the bark has no scent, it adds a nice texture to a woody blend. The tree is not harmed by having little curls pulled off, but you should never strip bark beyond the top papery layer.

Bougainvillea: Large papery blossoms in shades of pink. They have a very faint floral scent. These are surprisingly sturdy for their parchment transparency.

Calendula: Bright orange flowers that hold their color well when dried. They have no fragrance. Easily grown as an annual flower, they may be dried on wire screens or hung in bunches inside paper bags to catch the falling petals.

Chamomile: Tiny yellow flowers. They have a pungent, flowery scent. This is the same flower used in tea. The flowers fall apart easily but the scent remains.

Cardamom: White pods that are broken open to reveal small brown seeds. The seeds have a very strong, warm, spicy scent, good in spice or citrus-based blends.

◊ *Cedar:* Wood shavings of a reddish brown color. They have a strong, clean scent, used in woody blends and in moth-repellent potpourri. Cedar is most easily obtained in bags from pet supply stores. The tips of cedar branches, dried in a cool, shady place, can also be used, although their fragrance is less pungent.

Celosia: Feathery flowers in reds, oranges, and yellows. They have no fragrance. These plumes should be dried lying on their sides to hasten the process so they don't loose their color. Break the larger plumes apart for dashes of bright color.

◊ *Cinnamon:* The shaved bark of a tropical tree. Cinnamon has a rich, spicy fragrance. If possible, use soft stick cinnamon, which breaks up more easily, thereby releasing more of its fragrant oils. Harder sticks work best if they are broken into small pieces.

◊ *Clove:* Dark brown buds, very strongly scented. These are the same cloves used in cooking, but in their whole form, rather than ground to a powder.

Cones and pods: Small cones from balsam, hemlock, or other conifers add to bulk as well as appearance. Pods and seed heads of alder, eucalyptus, kazrina, and other trees or shrubs work just as well. They are especially appropriate in Christmas blends.

Coriander: Light brown seeds the size of peppercorns. Mildly spicy, they blend well with citrus and are more fragrant if they are broken slightly with a hammer.

Delphinium: Bright blue flowers with no scent. One of the few true blues that hold their color when dry, delphinium blossoms are a vibrant addition to potpourris using red or bright pink roses.

Dudinea: Small, translucent, buff-colored flowers. Although they appear fragile and delicate, these flowers are actually quite stiff. They provide air space in a potpourri while giving it a light, soft look.

Dusty miller: Gray, velvety leaves in deep-cut shapes. Although they have no scent, these leaves add a soft color and texture to potpourri, and are especially effective when pressed against the inside of a glass jar of bright flowers.

Eucalyptus: Long stiff leaves that blend well with nearly any flower.

Break the larger leaves into pieces to release their floral scent.

Elder flowers: Golden yellow with a sweet honey scent somewhat akin to orange blossoms. They are quite fine in texture and cannot be used for their color because they fall to the bottom.

Frankincense: A gum resin, available in small, rocklike lumps. Frankincense adds an oriental touch to any blend. It is often used in Christmas potpourri because it was one of the three gifts of the Wise Men.

Geranium: While the bright blossoms of the common house and garden plant dry well for a touch of color, it is the scented leaves of the pelargonium species of geranium that are used in potpourri. These vary from a deep, rich rose scent to a citrusy fragrance. The dried leaves are rarely available from suppliers, so it may be best to grow these yourself. They make very good houseplants, and are even more fragrant growing than they are when dried.

Globe amaranth: One of the brightest of the everlasting flowers, in magenta, pink, white, orange, and red. They look like clover blossoms and are as sturdy as they are colorful.

Heather: Tiny pink flowers with only a faint scent. They blend well with gray leaves, such as artemisia, for misty romantic blends.

Hibiscus: Dark red blossoms with a slightly sharp scent. They blend well with greens in a Christmas potpourri.

Holly berries: Round red berries that dry to a deep red. Most commonly used in Christmas blends.

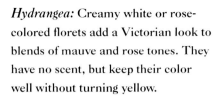

Hydrangea: Creamy white or rose-colored florets add a Victorian look to blends of mauve and rose tones. They have no scent, but keep their color well without turning yellow.

Jasmine: Delicate white flowers with a distinct floral scent. These add an oriental touch, usually boosted with a drop or two of jasmine oil.

Kazrina: Oval light brown pods with a prickly surface. Sizes range from one-half to two inches in diameter.

Lamb's ears: Pale green and velvety, with no scent. The smaller leaves of this herb add a soft texture and color to blends of rose and heather.

◊ *Lavender:* Tiny, but intensely fragrant purple blossoms. One of the few scents that will last for years without added oils, lavender has the clean, crisp smell we associate with freshly laundered linens. It is an invigorating scent that will dominate nearly any other in a potpourri. When purchasing lavender flowers, choose either the English or French—they have a brighter color and stronger scent than the Spanish.

Lemon marigold: Small, bright yellow blossoms with a light lemon scent. They add color and fragrance, and hold together well when dry.

Lemon peel: Yellow, very fragrant peel from common grocery-store lemons. Remove the peel with a potato peeler before squeezing the juice from the lemon for kitchen use. These form delicate curls as they dry.

◊ *Lemon verbena:* Green leaves with a strong lemon scent. This is the only plant that retains a true lemon fragrance when dried.

Marjoram: The variety used in potpourri is the barely-scented pot marjoram, also known as wild oregano. It is used primarily for its pink flowers, which dry to a rich rose color, although its leaves may also be used. Blossoms blend especially well in combinations of roses and artemisia.

◊ *Mint:* Green, highly fragrant leaves. There are several varieties of mint, each with its own distinctive scent. Spearmint is perhaps the strongest member of the mint family, with a clean, fresh smell; orange mint has a definite orange tone; and its close relative, eau-de-cologne mint, has a flowery scent.

Myrrh: Brown and resinous, with an oriental scent. It is also a fixative for other fragrances, a boon to those who have allergic reactions to orris root. As one of the gifts of the Wise Men, it has a place in Christmas blends, as well.

Oakmoss: Gray, with an earthy fragrance. Use moss in woody blends or where its gray color combines well with soft dusty pinks. It acts as a mild fixative for other scents.

Orange blossom: Creamy brown in color, with a rich honey scent. The blossoms give a heavy, intoxicating aura to potpourri if used in a large quantity.

◊ *Orange peel:* Deep orange color, with a sweet, fruity fragrance. Save the peel from fresh oranges and cut it into small pieces with scissors. Spread on a mesh screen or paper towels to dry quickly, or it will mildew.

◊ ***Orris root:*** The dried root of the Florentine iris, orris root is used as a fixative. Orris has almost no smell of its own, but has the remarkable quality of enhancing and holding the fragrances of other ingredients. Use it chipped, not powdered, for longer effectiveness as well as for aesthetic reasons. Powdered orris clings to flowers, leaves, and the inside of the jar, giving an overall dusty look. While orris in any form may produce allergic reactions in some people, even those without allergies will find orris powder irritating to their nose and eyes.

Pearly everlasting: Small, round, soft blossoms in pure white. They grow in clusters that can be used whole or broken into individual flowers.

Peppermint: Dark green leaves with a cooling menthol fragrance. Peppermint helps freshen an overly sweet blend, but should be used sparingly to keep it from overpowering lighter fragrances.

Pinks (Dianthus) and Carnations: Both are shades of pink, with a slightly spicy fragrance. These are the flowers from which the large ornamental carnation developed. Carnations dry well, too, but retain almost no fragrance.

◊ ***Rose:*** Pinks and reds, with a strong, lasting floral scent. Along with lavender, roses are the most common flower used in potpourri. Although hybrid, everblooming roses can be dried for their appearance, it is the June-blooming old-fashioned roses that have the best fragrance when dried. They can be picked as tight buds or left to form flowers before drying. The leaves retain their deep

green color when dried and may also be added to potpourri.

◊ *Rosemary:* Green, shaped like pine needles, with a distinctive herb smell. The strong fragrance blends well with flowers, especially roses.

Safflower: Bright orange threads with no scent. Although these have the color and look of Spanish saffron, they do not have the same flavor or scent as the herb. They are used strictly for their color.

Sandalwood: Pungent wood chips with an oriental flair. It blends well with other woods or with frankincense and myrrh, as well as heavy floral scents such as jasmine and orange blossom.

Star anise: A dark brown star-shaped spice with shiny seeds and a distinct anise scent. Used for its interesting shape and with rich spicy blends, especially those with orange.

Statice: Everlasting flower available in purple, blue, deep pink, peach, yellow, and white. Very brittle, the clusters of these bright flowers break quite easily. For a more dramatic effect in potpourri, try to keep clusters whole.

Strawflower: Stiff round blossoms that keep their shape well. Available in deep red, magenta, orange, yellow, white, and pink, these are a favorite of arrangers and potpourri makers alike. The vivid colors and variety of sizes can be used in nearly any blend. Place them carefully around the edge of a glass jar or scatter on top of a bowl of potpourri. Save the colorful petals of flowers that break apart and use these as well.

Sweet Annie: Dark brown, fine textured, and intensely fragrant. The fragile, feathery heads can also be bright green if they are picked early, but in either case they shatter to very fine seeds when dried.

Tansy: Yellow clusters of small button flowers, with a very slight acrid scent. The leaves of tansy are dried for use in moth-repellent potpourri blends, but are a little too strong for floral mixes.

Thyme: Tiny green leaves with a distinctly herbal scent. The same varieties of thyme used in the kitchen are also used in potpourri making. Their fragrance goes particularly well with roses and heather.

Tilia: Glossy, brown, star-shaped blossoms with a faint woody scent. They are used mostly for appearance.

Uva ursi: Tiny, oval, green leaves with no scent. They are used for their neat appearance and color, especially with tiny rosebuds, which would be hidden by larger green leaves.

Woodruff: Rich green, with a mild scent of new-mown hay. Woodruff is most commonly used as a fixative and to prevent musty odors. It is the best ingredient for a closet potpourri or for one to use in the bureau drawers of seasonal homes that are closed up for a portion of the year.

Yarrow: Flat yellow blossoms with no fragrance. The foliage has a sharp scent. The flowers are used for color, usually if broken into smaller segments. The variety of yarrow sold in natural food stores for cosmetic use is a different one; look for the yellow blossomed yarrow where ornamental dried flowers are sold.

Zinnia: Bright red, pink, yellow, orange, and white, with no fragrance. Flowers are showy, ranging in size from one inch to three or four inches. They hold together well when dried and retain their bright colors. Use smaller blossoms whole and break larger ones into pieces.

Preserving the Fragrance

Once a potpourri smells and looks good, you must preserve and strengthen its scent. Orris is the best fixative, and should be used chipped, not powdered. It has no scent of its own, but helps preserve others.

Other fixatives, such as myrrh and sweet woodruff, help to prolong the fragrance of other ingredients, but orris root is the most commonly used.

Although the amount of fixative used will depend on the strength of the other ingredients, about a table-spoonful of orris for each cup of potpourri is usually about right.

Some ingredients, including spices, are strong and long-lasting enough to hold their scent without a fixative. But nearly any potpourri will last longer if one is used.

Fragrant Oils

In the process of drying herbs, blossoms, and foliage for use in potpourri, some of the fragrant oils evaporate, along with the moisture, and are lost. Essential oils, fragrant essences extracted from the plants, are often added to potpourri not only to strengthen the fragrance, but to make it last longer.

These oils are very concentrated (unless they have been "cut" with less expensive oils), and only a few drops are needed to boost the natural scents in a potpourri. It is better to spend more money for the best oils than to use diluted oils.

In choosing the oils to add, it is best to stay as close as possible to the ingredients in the potpourri. Some oils, such as rose and bay, will intensify and bring out the fragrance of other plants as well as their own. These are both good general purpose oils. Others, such as lavender and citrus oils, are distinctive and tend to predominate. Beginners who can purchase only one oil should choose rose, adding others as their repertoire of ingredients expands.

It is best to avoid fruit oils, except for citrus, since such fragrances as strawberry have a strong, artificial smell that becomes tiresome very quickly.

The amount of oil to use depends upon its strength, the amount of the potpourri, and the use for which it is intended. Potpourri that will be enclosed in small sachets need to be stronger in oils than those that will be in a large jar. Unlike enclosed blends, sachets are open to the air at all times, so the scent dissipates more quickly. Three or four drops per pint of plant material is usually about right for potpourri that will be in a covered container.

The oil may be dropped directly into the potpourri mixture or it can be mixed with chipped orris root first. The latter method assures that it will spread more evenly throughout the potpourri and also helps to preserve its fragrance longer.

When oils are first added to the potpourri, the mixture will have a raw, sharp smell. As it has a chance to blend it will mellow and become smoother. To help this process, a potpourri should be kept closed for at least two weeks after it is made, and stirred or shaken each day.

Balsam fir: Pungent and quite strong. Balsam fir oil should be used sparingly to boost the natural fragrance of balsam tips and needles. This oil also blends well with cedar, rose, or bay oils.

Bay: Mild and pleasant, with undertones of both spice and flowers. It blends well with nearly all other fragrances, especially spices, citrus, and woody mixtures.

Carnation: Spicy and floral at the same time. It blends well with roses, adding a crisp note to balance the sweetness of the rose.

Cedar: Very strong scent, but blends well with other oils. Use it in woody or spice combinations, Christmas blends, and moth-preventive potpourri. It balances well with both balsam and citrus oils.

Cinnamon: Very strong and spicy. Use it sparingly and only in fairly large volumes of potpourri where it can be one of several oils. It blends well with citrus and adds life to woody potpourri.

Frankincense: Warm and pungent with an oriental flavor. It combines well with spices and other oriental fragrances, as well as citrus and rose. Use it in Christmas blends.

Gardenia: Heady and sweet. The fragrance of gardenia blossoms, along with their fragile waxy color, is lost in drying. But used sparingly, the oil adds a tropical, floral note to oriental mixtures.

Honeysuckle: Sweet and heavy, this is another one to use sparingly. It blends well with floral mixtures, especially if crisper scents such as lemon are used.

Hyacinth: Light floral scent, fresher than most florals. It is light enough to be used in woody blends.

Jasmine: Heavy and sweet, jasmine is perhaps the most seductive of all. Balance it with oriental fragrances and a little rose oil.

Lavender: Fresh and clean, slightly sharp. One of the strongest of the oils, lavender is best used with rose or other more subtle fragrances. Lavender oil is a favorite in sachets because of its endurance.

Lemon: Rich and fruity, but fresh. Blend this with orange or bay in spicy mixtures or to add a crisp touch to florals. It can also be used to lighten the fragrances of a woody blend.

Lily of the valley: Sweet and haunting, a little strong if used alone. Mix with rose, bay, or even carnation to soften it. Use it in blends of pastel-colored spring flowers.

Orange: Sweet and spicy, a little too heavy to use alone. Lemon helps cut down its sweetness, balancing it nicely. Use in tropical blends as well as mixtures of spices and woods.

Orange blossom: Floral with a strong hint of honey. Use in tropical and oriental blends.

Rose: Light, sweet, and floral. This is the most universal of all the oils; it is hard to imagine a potpourri that wouldn't be improved by it. Blend with other florals or use it to soften sharper scents such as lavender or cedar. Use it to refresh a tired potpourri.

Sandalwood: Exotic and slightly spicy. Use in any blend for an oriental flavor. It mixes well with other woods, spices, and some of the more exotic florals.

Mixing Potpourri

There is no magic to mixing the ingredients, and no particular order in which they should be added. A large glass or pottery bowl is a good container for blending. White or a light color makes it easier to see what the colors look like together, but that is not essential.

If you are following a recipe exactly, you can mix the entire batch at once, adding the amount specified for each ingredient. But if you are creating a blend of your own, you might want to begin by mixing in a spoonful of each to see how all of the elements look and smell together. If you like the combination you can add more, but if you don't, you won't have

used a lot of ingredients. Also, if one scent seems to overpower the others, you can dilute it by adding more of other flowers or herbs in the blend.

When you have made a blend that you like, mix it well and seal in a jar with plenty of air space. Shake or stir it daily for two weeks to allow it to blend and ripen. After that, your potpourri is ready to display and enjoy.

Displaying Your Potpourri

The best containers for potpourri are those that can be left open so the fragrance fills the room, then closed so that the blend can recoup its scent. Special jars are made for this purpose, but any container with a cover will do just as well. Open bowls or cups will also work as long as they are covered with a plate, saucer, or even plastic wrap for a few hours each day.

Clear glass apothecary jars are perfect for showing off a beautiful combination of flowers, as are round rose bowls (available in florists' shops) and large brandy snifters. Covered glass candy dishes make elegant containers; a kitchen potpourri of spices is at home in an old-fashioned, glass-domed canning jar.

If you are using a china container (odd sugar bowls make especially good potpourri jars), try to find one that blends well with the theme or colors of the potpourri. You can adapt the ingredients to suit the container.

Search tag sales, bazaars, and flea markets. With a little imagination, you will soon see containers in everything from a teacup whose saucer is long gone to a tall parfait glass.

While baskets generally allow too much air flow, causing a potpourri to lose its scent rather quickly, some stronger blends can be displayed in these. A Christmas blend rich in spices and balsam will last the holiday season without having to be covered each night.

Wooden boxes, especially oval Shaker-style ones, show off potpourri beautifully and have the added advantage of a cover. These are good containers for potpourri that will be shipped to someone far away.

Also easy to mail are flexible lucite boxes, although they are hard to find. You can dress these up by placing whole flowers on the top in a nice arrangement.

Glass, pottery, wood, china, or plastic are all good materials for containers. Round cardboard boxes work well as long as they are treated inside with a clear sealer to keep the cardboard from absorbing the oils. Do not use metal containers because they will react badly with the oils and give the potpourri an unpleasant smell.

Sachets

Potpourri blends that will be stitched into sachets do not need to be beautiful. This is the place to use the less colorful petals. These blends are best without bulky ingredients; small, highly fragrant flowers and herbs are best. Lavender, rose petals, lemon verbena, and spices are good in sachets. A little extra oil and orris root helps make up for the fact that only a little bit of the blend will be used in each sachet.

To make a sachet, use any natural fabric. Softer, loosely woven ones allow the scent to spread better. Choose a fabric to match the mood of the contents: wool, burlap, or muslin for homey spice and wool blends with cedar or balsam, and dainty laces and chintzes for lavender- and rose-based florals.

Caring for Your Potpourri

To make potpourri last longer, keep it covered as many hours a day as it is open. Many people close the jar or cover the dish at night, opening it each morning. Try to keep the blend out of the sun, which will cause it to fade and the scent to dissipate. If the fragrance does fade, simply treat it as you would a brand new mix—add orris root and oil and let it blend in a large jar for two weeks.

You can do the same thing to an old potpourri that you did not make yourself. If you can tell by looking at it what its main fragrant ingredients are, add oils to match them. If you are not sure what its ingredients are, use rose or bay oil for a floral blend, jasmine or sandalwood for an oriental blend, and cinnamon or orange for a spice blend.

P·O·T·P·O·U·R·R·I R·E·C·I·P·E·S

Lavender and Old Lace

1 cup lavender
¼ cup delphinium blossoms
¼ cup white strawflower petals
½ cup small, white globe amaranth
A few individual flowers of pearly everlasting
1 small, perfect white strawflower (may be tinged with pink)
2 tablespoons orris root chips
4 to 5 drops lavender oil

Whites in shades from creamy to silvery set off the rich blues and purples of this somewhat formal blend. You can substitute other small white flowers, but the blue of delphinium looks better here than statice. This is a fairly strong blend that can be left uncovered for several days at a time.

Display it with the perfect strawflower in the center of the top.

Lavender and Rose

1 cup lavender
1 cup dark pink rosebuds
½ cup delphinium blossoms
2 tablespoons orris root chips
2 drops lavender oil
2 drops rose oil

There are few simpler potpourris, and none more beautiful or fragrant. Although it is strong enough to last in a sachet, it is far too rich and beautiful to hide.

Display it in clear glass or a simple antique bowl of Chinese blueware.

Lura's Lavender

1 cup lavender
½ cup dark purple statice
¼ cup delphinium
¼ cup red roses
¼ cup allspice ·
1 tablespoon cloves
1 tablespoon calendula
A few pink zinnias
2 tablespoons orris root chips
2 to 3 drops lavender oil
3 to 4 drops rose oil

Created by a little girl too young to read a recipe, this delights the senses of anyone who loves the color purple and the fragrance of lavender.

Display it in a pure white container or small wicker basket.

Green and Gold

½ cup lemon verbena
½ cup small bright yellow and gold strawflowers
¼ cup bright yellow strawflower petals
¼ cup yellow statice blossoms
¼ cup tansy and/or yarrow flowers
¼ cup calendula
¼ cup lemon marigolds
¼ cup rose leaves
2 tablespoons uva ursi leaves
3 tablespoons orris root chips
5 to 6 drops lemon oil
2 to 3 drops honeysuckle oil

An unusual potpourri, this contains none of the "old standby" ingredients for fragrance: rose, lavender, spices, or woods. The flowers and leaves are chosen instead for their color; only the lemon verbena has a noticeable fragrance.

Christmas Blend

1 cup red rosebuds
1 cup short balsam tips and needles
1 cup hemlock cones
½ cup broken stick cinnamon
½ cup allspice
½ cup orange peel
2 tablespoons cloves
6 to 8 broken bay leaves
¼ cup holly berries

◊ ◊ ◊ ◊ ◊

There is no oil or orris root in this fragrant combination. The balsam needles, spices, and roses will keep their scent throughout the holidays, but if you think they could use a little help, add orris with rose, balsam, and orange oils.

Christmas Basket

3 to 4 large pinecones
½ cup red carnations, whole
5 to 6 medium cones or dark pods
1 cup balsam tips
½ cup holly berries
5 to 6 cinnamon sticks, 4 to 6 inches long
½ cup allspice

You can break the rule about dried ingredients with this one, using fresh balsam tips and holly berries. The berries and allspice should be sprinkled over the rest of the blend after it is arranged, so they will stick in between the petals of the cones. The balsam will remain fragrant throughout the entire season, but you can boost the other scents with a drop or two of carnation oil if you wish.

Arrange this bold mixture in a dark basket or wooden bowl.

Christmas Spice

¼ *cup frankincense*
¼ *cup myrrh*
¼ *cup broken cinnamon*
¼ *cup allspice*
2 tablespoons cloves
½ *cup red rosebuds*

◊ ◊ ◊ ◊ ◊

Simplicity itself, with two of the Magi's gifts, three spices from the East, and the red roses of martyrdom, this needs no oil or orris.

Present it in small gold net bags or in clear boxes tied with a gold cord and a tag explaining its ingredients.

(*Photo on previous page.*)

Spring Flowers

½ cup white or light pink strawflowers

½ cup white or light pink globe amaranth

½ cup dudinea or other buff-colored flowers

½ cup pink roses

½ cup bougainvillea

¼ cup uva ursi leaves

¼ cup lemon verbena

¼ cup broken eucalyptus leaves

A few purple and white acrolinium

A few sprigs of blue statice

1 tablespoon sweet woodruff

1 tablespoon allspice

1 teaspoon cloves

3 tablespoons orris root chips

5 drops rose oil

2 drops hyacinth oil

The faint pungence of spices sets off the sweetness of flowers. The acrolinium can be left out or can replace the strawflowers. Add any other pastel blossoms that are available.

Summer Scents

1 cup mixed petals and leaves (whatever is most abundant in your garden)
½ cup whole carnations
1 cup small whole strawflowers
¼ cup statice flowers
¼ cup rose petals
3 to 4 eucalyptus leaves, broken
¼ cup lemon verbena
¼ cup calendula
¼ cup scented geranium leaves
4 tablespoons orris root chips
3 to 4 drops carnation oil
3 to 4 drops rose oil
1 drop lemon oil

Richer in color and fragrance than the spring garden flowers, this potpourri represents summer at its fullest. Try for a real variety of colors as you collect the blossoms.

Display the blend with the small strawflowers on top or around the sides of a glass container.

Autumn Woods

½ cup hemlock or other very small cones

½ cup lemon verbena

¼ cup calendula

¼ cup orange and yellow strawflower petals

½ cup balsam needles

½ cup cedar shavings

¼ cup broken cinnamon

¼ cup uva ursi

8 to 10 bay leaves

3 tablespoons orris root chips

2 to 3 drops balsam fir oil

2 to 3 drops cedar oil

2 to 3 drops bay oil

1 drop lemon oil

The colors of autumn and the spicy, earthy smell of the woods will last all year with this lively blend.

Serve it up to be admired in a wooden bowl or box or in an old canning jar.

Winter Spice

¼ cup tilia flowers
¼ cup broken cinnamon
¼ cup allspice
¼ cup coriander
¼ cup orange peel
2 tablespoons cloves
2 tablespoons cardamom seeds

Although the spices in this are expensive, the rich fragrance will last all winter without orris or oils. Keep this in a jar in the kitchen or simmer a little of it on the back of the stove. To restore this blend when it has become tired, rinse it quickly in very hot water, spread it on a baking sheet, and dry it in a slow oven.

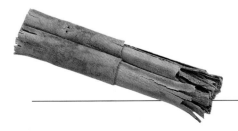

Sweet and Gold

¼ cup elder flowers
¼ cup sweet Annie tops
¼ cup chamomile
1 tablespoon cardamom seeds
1 tablespoon tansy buttons
¼ cup individual yellow statice florets, cut from stems
A pinch of safflower
1 tablespoon powdered orris (optional)

Sweet with just a hint of spice, the texture of this blend is too fine to display it in large quantities, where it would pack down. There is no orris and no oil, so enjoy this one while it lasts, then add it to another mixture. Orris root would stand out as white chunks in this, so use powdered orris if you want to use a fixative.

Country House Chintz

½ cup bougainvillea
½ cup white hydrangea
½ cup white globe amaranth
10 to 12 small bay leaves
¼ cup uva ursi
2 tablespoons calendula
¼ cup yellow statice, broken apart
2 tablespoons orris root chips
3 to 4 drops bay oil
2 to 3 drops hyacinth oil

Bold in design, but subtle in its colors, this chintz pattern lets the rose predominate against a creamy background and dusty green leaves. Few potpourris combine pinks with highlights of yellow—and none does it with such charm.

Cottage Garden

2 cups mixed garden flowers in all colors, large flowers broken
1 cup mixed foliage
¼ cup lemon verbena
¼ cup bay leaves
¼ cup calendula
½ cup roses
4 tablespoons orris root chips
4 to 5 drops rose oil
2 drops bay oil
2 drops hyacinth oil
1 drop lemon oil

There is nothing sparing about this eclectic blend of whatever is in bloom. No theme or color predominates; if the colors seem heavy in one direction, add statice florets in other colors to balance it. Mix this all summer long, adding more flowers as they bloom and dry. When you have a combination of colors you like, add the orris and oil.

(Photo on previous page.)

Edwardian Lace

½ cup bougainvillea
½ cup dudinea
½ cup large pink rosebuds
½ cup white and light pink globe amaranth
½ cup white hydrangea
2 tablespoons orris root chips
3 to 4 drops rose oil
2 to 3 drops lily of the valley oil
1 drop hyacinth oil

◊ ◊ ◊ ◊ ◊

Unabashedly feminine, this blend of translucent petals appears light enough to drift away on the slightest breeze.

Display it in very thin china with a wispy, delicate pattern, or less formally in a cream-colored painted wicker basket.

Victorian Garden

1 cup bougainvillea
1 cup deep red strawflowers
1 cup purple globe amaranth
1 cup dark red celosia
½ cup purple statice
½ cup whole red roses
¼ cup orris root chips
5 to 6 drops rose oil
3 to 4 drops gardenia oil

Big, bold, and a little florid, the deep colors of whole roses and strawflowers are broken only by the transparency of the bougainvillea.

Nothing is understated here, so show it off in a flamboyant or heavily cut glass punch bowl.

Sweet Innocence

¼ cup tiny, perfect pink rosebuds
½ cup tiny white flowers, such as acrolinium or globe amaranth
2 tablespoons white hydrangea
2 tablespoons baby's breath sprigs
1 tablespoon heather
1 tablespoon rosemary
1 tablespoon orris root chips
2 drops rose oil

Choose only the tiniest and most perfect blossoms in pink and creamy whites. This is no place for loose petals or overblown flowers. Since these miniatures are rare, this makes only a little.

Oriental Garden

½ cup red rosebuds
½ cup dark pink rosebuds
½ cup broken cinnamon
¼ cup tilia flowers
¼ cup hibiscus flowers
¼ cup myrrh
¼ cup orange blossoms
¼ cup jasmine flowers
2 tablespoons cloves
2 tablespoons cardamom seeds
2 tablespoons star anise
2 tablespoons sandalwood chips
2 to 3 drops jasmine oil
2 to 3 drops rose oil
1 to 2 drops sandalwood oil

Rich dark colors and a distinctly oriental fragrance mark this heady blend.

Display it in an open oriental bowl decorated in rich colors. This is not a potpourri for a white or pastel container or a dainty tea cup.

Woodsong

½ cup cedar shavings
½ cup hemlock or other very small cones
¼ cup balsam needles
¼ cup calendula
¼ cup tilia flowers
¼ cup broken cinnamon
¼ cup yarrow and/or tansy
¼ cup elder flowers
A few alder cones
2 tablespoons orris root chips
2 to 3 drops cedar oil
1 to 2 drops balsam oil
1 drop sandalwood oil
¼ cup uva ursi (optional)
¼ cup bittersweet berries (optional)

A woody blend for any season, the bittersweet and uva ursi add a bright accent of orange and the softening touch of green.

Display it in an earthy bowl.

Forest and Flowers

½ cup cedar shavings
½ cup balsam tips and needles
½ cup pink rosebuds
½ cup hemlock cones
¼ cup lemon verbena
¼ cup oakmoss
A few curls of birchbark
A few alder cones
2 tablespoons sweet Annie
3 tablespoons orris root chips
2 to 3 drops balsam fir oil
2 to 3 drops cedar oil
2 to 3 drops rose oil

Wild roses on a stone wall, fir trees in the summer sun—this blend says New England. Add whatever native wildflowers are available: lupine, Queen Anne's lace, goldenrod, or others.

Valentine

½ cup red roses
½ cup dark purple statice
2 tablespoons delphinium blossoms
1 tablespoon pure white strawflower petals
1 tablespoon lavender
1 tablespoon orris root chips
4 drops rose oil
1 drop jasmine oil

◊ ◊ ◊ ◊ ◊

Heady with deep red roses and purple flowers with just a breath of seductive jasmine, there is no innocence in this potpourri.

It deserves to be presented in a crystal dish, but a heart-shaped candy box will do. (*Photo on previous page.*)

Highland Heather

½ cup heather
½ cup pink rose petals
¼ cup rosemary
¼ cup artemisia
¼ cup oakmoss
¼ cup uva ursi
¼ cup broken eucalyptus leaves
¼ cup dusty miller or small lamb's-ear leaves
3 tablespoons orris root chips
4 to 5 drops rose oil
1 to 2 drops hyacinth oil

The misty colors of gray-green foliage set off the dusty pinks of the flowers in this gentle blend. You can add other soft pink flowers or gray foliage such as zinnia petals and the leaves of lavender, whose subtle scent blends well with roses and heather.

(*Photo on page 6.*)

Serengeti

½ cup acacia leaves and tips
½ cup tilia flowers
¼ cup myrrh
¼ cup kazrina
2 tablespoons broken cinnamon

◊   ◊   ◊   ◊   ◊

The dusty fragrance of East Africa's thorn tree, with myrrh from Ethiopia and a breath of Zanzibar cinnamon, makes this a subtle potpourri anyone could live with. There are no oils or orris, nothing flowery or feminine, just the faint scent that hangs in the African air, sparse as the bushveld and just as haunting.

Irish Tweed

½ *cup oakmoss*
½ *cup cedar shavings*
¼ *cup heather*
¼ *cup lavender*
¼ *cup rosemary*
¼ *cup lemon verbena*
¼ *cup kazrina pods or other small cones*
2 tablespoons uva ursi
2 tablespoons acacia leaves and tips
2 tablespoons chamomile
2 tablespoons orris root chips
2 drops cedar oil
1 drop lavender oil

Rugged, roughcut, and a little prickly, this is an outdoor blend, reminiscent of mist and hedgerows. Its crispness is warmed by a touch of sweet chamomile.

Moth Buster

1 cup cedar shavings
½ cup lavender
½ cup lemon verbena
½ cup rosemary
¼ cup pennyroyal
¼ cup spearmint or peppermint
¼ cup broken cinnamon
¼ cup cloves
¼ cup black peppercorns
¼ cup sweet Annie
10 to 12 bay leaves, broken
¼ cup coriander
¼ cup orris root chips
4 to 5 drops cedar oil
3 to 4 drops lavender oil
3 to 4 drops lemon oil

A no-nonsense blend used before the days of chemical moth preparations, this has a pleasant fresh scent. Other ingredients reputed to discourage moths are southernwood, lemon peel, tansy, and yarrow.

Package this in fairly large bags, perhaps made of wool.

Sources

Herbitage Farm
686 Old Homestead Highway
Richmond, NH 03470
Mixed dried flowers, cones, and pods (catalog $1.00)

Maine Balsam Fir Products
P.O. Box 123
West Paris, ME 04289
Fragrant balsam needles

Aphrodisia
282 Bleeker Street
New York, NY 10014
Complete line of potpourri ingredients, supplies, and containers (informative catalog $2.00)